Counting Animals
I Count Three

T0025131

By Julia Jaske

 I count three pigs.

I count three sheep.

I count three horses.

I count three chickens.

I count three cows.

I count three cheetahs.

I count three rabbits.

I count three deer.

 I count three goats.

I count three sharks.

I count three owls.

I count three koalas.

Word List

pigs	cows	goats
sheep	cheetahs	sharks
horses	rabbits	owls
chickens	deer	koalas

48 Words

I count three pigs.
I count three sheep.
I count three horses.
I count three chickens.
I count three cows.
I count three cheetahs.
I count three rabbits.
I count three deer.
I count three goats.
I count three sharks.
I count three owls.
I count three koalas.

CHERRY BLOSSOM PRESS

Published in the United States of America by Cherry Lake Publishing
Ann Arbor, Michigan
www.cherrylakepublishing.com

Photo Credits: ©Henk Bentlage/Shutterstock.com, front cover; ©Jason Boyce/Shutterstock.com, 1; ©Simun Ascic/Shutterstock.com, 2; ©TheOldhiro/Shutterstock.com, 3; ©Kwadrat/Shutterstock.com, 4; ©Nataliia Reshetnikova/Shutterstock.com, 5; ©Clara Bastian/Shutterstock.com, 6; ©Ondrej Prosicky/Shutterstock.com, 7; ©Serenko Natalia/Shutterstock.com, 8; ©Vlad Sokolovsky/Shutterstock.com, 9; ©Andrew Mayovskyy/Shutterstock.com, 10; ©Sail Far Dive Deep/Shutterstock.com, 11; ©YuenSiuTien/Shutterstock.com, 12; ©Ekaterina Kamenetsky/Shutterstock.com, 13; ©Krakenimages.com/Shutterstock.com, 15

Cherry Blossom Press is an imprint of Cherry Lake Publishing Group.

Library of Congress Cataloging-in-Publication Data
Names: Jaske, Julia, author.
Title: I count three / Julia Jaske.
Description: Ann Arbor, Michigan : Cherry Lake Publishing, [2020] | Series: Counting animals | Audience: Ages 4-6. | Summary: "Look! How many animals do you see? The Counting Animals series uses exciting and familiar animals to support early readers quest to count. The simple text makes it easy for children to engage in reading, and uses the Whole Language approach to literacy, a combination of sight words and repetition that builds recognition and confidence. Bold, colorful photographs correlate directly to the text to help guide readers through the book"— Provided by publisher.
Identifiers: LCCN 2020003010 (print) | LCCN 2020003011 (ebook) | ISBN 9781534168367 (paperback) | ISBN 9781534171886 (pdf) | ISBN 9781534173729 (ebook)
Subjects: LCSH: Counting—Juvenile literature. | Animals—Miscellanea—Juvenile literature.
Classification: LCC QA113 .J39 2020 (print) | LCC QA113 (ebook) | DDC 513.2/1—dc23
LC record available at https://lccn.loc.gov/2020003010
LC ebook record available at https://lccn.loc.gov/2020003011

Cherry Lake Publishing Group would like to acknowledge the work of the Partnership for 21st Century Learning, a Network of Battelle for Kids. Please visit http://www.battelleforkids.org/networks/p21 for more information.

Printed in the United States of America
Corporate Graphics